Paleo Bread

Healthy Delicious Gluten Free Bread, Biscuits, Muffins, Waffles & Pancakes Cookbook!

Disclaimer

While the author has made every effort to ensure that the ideas, guidelines and information presented in this Book are safe, they should be used at the reader's discretion. The author cannot be held responsible for any personal or commercial damage arising from the application or misinterpretation of information presented herein.

Table of Contents

Introduction

I want to thank you and congratulate you for purchasing the book, "**Paleo Bread - Healthy Delicious Gluten Free Bread, Biscuits, Muffins, Waffles & Pancakes Cookbook!**"

This book contains proven steps and strategies on how to bake and cook healthy gluten free bread while on a Paleo Diet.

Most people planning to try Paleo Diet lament about having to give up eating bread. Bread is a staple food for everybody in the world. While on Paleo, most bread is prohibited in the diet because a lot of them are made from wheat and grains. Besides, cavemen did not eat flour based food back then nor did they know how to bake.

The Paleo Diet, if done strict to the rules, will only require you to eat foods that are present during the hunter-gatherer period. Most of the recommended food consists of natural and organic meat, fruits and greens. The simple the process you make to the food, the more Paleo you go.

Because bread has been an integral part of every man's meal, 'netizens' on Paleo have come up with creative ways to make bread using Paleo-approved ingredients. This means, people on Paleo can still eat bread without the wheat, grains and dairy by using alternative flours from nuts and seeds. This means, you can still enjoy a slice of bread or two without feeling guilty.

This book will help you prepare, bake and cook gluten-free and dairy free Paleo bread, waffles, pancakes, biscuits and muffins in quick and easy steps.

Thanks again for purchasing this book. I hope you enjoy it!

Chapter 1. Classic Paleo Bread Recipes

Cavemen didn't have ovens or microwaves back then, but if they did, they would have loved to whip up some of these breads. The good thing about bread is you can make a meal in a just few seconds and go about your day.

 When on strict Paleo, commercial bread made form wheat grains and dairy are a no-no. However with these recipes made from Paleo approved ingredients, you can still enjoy bread. You can make these over the weekend, store the loaves in the fridge and just pop it out to make a toast or a cold-cut sandwich using stuffing and condiments conforming to the Paleo Diet.

Simple Paleo Bread Recipe
(Makes 1 loaf, Prep for 10 minutes, Bake for an hour)

Ingredients:

3	cups	of almond flour
¼	cup	almond milk or tap water
3	pcs	organic eggs
1	tsp	sodium bicarbonate or baking soda
2	tsp	baking powder
½	cup	coconut oil or olive oil
¼	tsp	salt

Instructions:

1. Preheat the oven up to 300 F°.
2. Grease a 9"x5"loaf pan with coconut oil or olive oil.
3. Combine all the remaining ingredients together in a large- sized bowl to create a batter.
4. Slowly pour the almond flour batter onto the pan. Spread the batter evenly until the whole pan is covered.
5. Bake the basic Paleo bread for an hour.
6. Remove from the oven and let it cool. Flip the pan, and use a bread knife to slice.

4-Flour Paleo Bread With Sunflower Seed Toppings

(Makes 1 loaf or 12 slices, Prep for 10 minutes, Bake for an hour)

Ingredients:

Dry

½	cup	of coconut flour
1 ½	cup	of almond flour
¼	cup	flaxseed meal
½	cup	tapioca flour
½	tsp	cream of tartar
½	tsp	sea salt
1	tsp	sodium bicarbonate or baking soda
¼	cup	raw sunflower seeds (for toppings)

Wet

1	cup	melted coconut oil (½ for greasing and ½ for the batter)
½	cup	of coconut milk (full fat)
1	tsp	vinegar (apple cider)
4	pcs	free-range eggs

Instructions:

1. Preheat the oven up to 350°F.
2. Use the melted coconut oil to grease an 8½" x 4½" loaf pan.
3. Mix all the dry ingredients except the sunflower seeds in a large- sized bowl until everything is well incorporated. Sift the dry ingredients if deemed necessary.
4. Using a separate bowl, whisk all the wet ingredients together with the eggs.
5. Pour the wet ingredients over the dry ingredients. Gently mix them together using a wooden or rubber spatula until a thick batter is created. Avoid over mixing.
6. Pour the batter in to the greased loaf pan and spread evenly. Sprinkle the sunflower seeds on top.
7. Bake in the oven for about 40 to 45 minutes. To determine if the bread is cooked, insert a toothpick in the center of the bread. If it comes out clean, it's cooked.
8. Remove from the oven and let cool before slicing into desired number.

Paleo Quick Microwave Bread

(Makes 4 small round slices, Prep for 4 minutes, Cook for 5 minutes)

Ingredients

⅓	cup	of almond flour
1	tbsp	of coconut flour or chia bran
1	pc	free-range egg, whisked
½	tsp	baking powder
2 ½	tbsp	ghee or coconut oil, melted (use ½ tbsp for greasing)
⅛	tsp	sea salt

Instructions:

1. Grease a mug with ghee or coconut oil.
2. Put all the ingredients in a bowl and mix them using a fork.
3. After everything blended evenly, pour them into the mug.
4. Put the mug in a microwave and set the timer on high for 90 seconds.
5. Remove from the microwave and let it cool.
6. Gently pop the bread out of the mug and slice.

Almond And Chestnut Flour Paleo Bread

(Makes 1 small loaf or 8 slices, prep for 5 minutes, Cook for 25 minutes)

Ingredients:

¼	cup	ground almonds or almond flour
¼	cup	tbsp chestnut flour
3	tbsp	of coconut flour
3	pcs	free-range eggs, whisked
¾	cup	of coconut milk
¼	cup	arrowroot
½	tsp	sodium bicarbonate or baking soda
¼	tsp	salt
½	tsp	coconut oil, for greasing

Instructions:

1. Preheat the oven up to 350°F
2. Use a coconut oil to grease a loaf pan.
3. In a bowl, beat the eggs and pour the milk. Whisk.
4. In a separate large bowl, add in all the dry ingredients. Pour the whisked eggs and milk and mix them all together with a wooden spatula until a batter is formed.
5. Pour the bread batter onto the greased pan.
6. Bake in the oven for 25 minutes. Use the toothpick test to make sure that the center of the bread is cooked.
7. Let cool before slicing.

Cashew Paleo Buns

(Makes 6 buns, Prep for 10 minutes, Cook for 30 minutes)

Ingredients:

¼	cup	of coconut flour
½	cup	tapioca flour
½	cup	raw cashews
½	tsp	baking powder
½	tsp	sea salt
½	tsp	vinegar (apple cider)
2	pcs	large eggs, whisked
½	cup	water

Instructions:

1. Preheat oven at 350°F.
2. Using a food processor or blender, grind the cashew nuts until it turns into flour.
3. Combine all the dry ingredients in a large- sized bowl.
4. Beat all the wet ingredients in a separate bowl and pour over the bowl with the dry ingredients.
5. Mix thoroughly until the batter is well blended.
6. Pour the bread batter into a greased hamburger bun pan.
7. Bake the buns in the oven for about 25 - 30 minutes.
8. Remove from oven. Let it cool before slicing the buns in half.

Paleo Sandwich Bread

(Makes 1 loaf, Prep for 10 minutes, Cook for an hour)

Ingredients:

Dry

¼	cup	of coconut flour
1	tsp	sodium bicarbonate or baking soda
½	tsp	sea salt

Wet

¼	cup	almond milk
1	cup	cashew butter, melted
4	pcs	large eggs, separated
2 ½	tsp	vinegar
2	tbsp	honey

Instructions:

1. Set your oven to 300°F. To achieve a white colored loaf, put a small dish with water at the bottom rack.
2. Use a parchment paper to line the bottom of an 8.5×4.5 loaf pan (preferably glass). Grease the sides of the pan with coconut oil.
3. Beat the egg yolks with the cashew butter before adding the vinegar, milk and honey. Use an electric hand beater or a mixer to avoid sticking.
4. In a separate bowl, beat the egg whites with an electric hand mixer until it peaks.
5. In a medium sized bowl, combine all the dry ingredients. Mix thoroughly.
6. Pour the bowl of wet ingredients into the dry ingredient's bowl and beat everything until it's all combined.
7. Pour the beaten egg whites into the mixture and mix again until everything is well incorporated. Avoid over mixing.
8. Pour all of the bread's batter into the lined and greased loaf pan.
9. Bake in the oven for 40-45 minutes until golden brown. Use the toothpick test to make sure the center is cooked.
10. Remove from the oven and let cool for 20 minutes.
11. Free the sides of the pan using a knife before flipping it upside down into the cooling rack.

Chapter 2. Spiced-up Paleo Bread Recipes

You can keep Paleo baking fun with these creative recipes for bread. Adding more novelty to bread makes dieting much more fun and exciting while keeping your health on track and your waistline thin. These Paleo bread recipes can accompany any salad, meat dish or a complementary smack to a brunch or an afternoon cup of tea.

If you get bored with plain sandwiches for breakfast and lunch, try these leveled-up Paleo bread recipes to fill your day. Most are complemented by fruits, vegetables and Paleo approved flours and starches like almond flour, coconut flour, flax seed and others. Just remember that it's more Paleo if you use only fresh, natural and organic ingredients.

Paleo Banana-Pumpkin Bread

(Makes 1 loaf, Prep for 10 minutes, Cook for 30 minutes)

Ingredients:

Dry
1	cup	of almond flour
1	cup	pumpkins boiled and pureed
½	pc	medium banana, mashed
4	pcs	medium dates, pitted
½	cup	almond butter
¼	tsp	ginger, ground
1	tbsp	cinnamon
½	tsp	nutmeg
¼	cup	pecans, chopped

A dash of sea salt

Wet
¼	tbsp	of coconut oil (use it for greasing)
1	tsp	vanilla extract
¼	cup	pure maple syrup
4	pcs	large organic eggs

Instructions:

1. Set oven at 350°F.
2. Combine banana, boiled pumpkin, almond butter, maple syrup, eggs, dates and vanilla into a blender or a food processor. Pulse until mixture turns smooth.
3. Add the almond flour, nutmeg, cinnamon, salt and ginger. Pulse on high until the batter thickens.
4. Mix in the pecans in the batter.
5. Grease a medium sized loaf pan with coconut oil. Pour the batter and spread evenly.
6. Bake the batter for 30 minutes. Do the toothpick test to test if cooked.
7. Let cool and slice to desired thickness.

Sweet Potato Raisin Bread

(Makes 1 loaf, Prep for 10 minutes, Cook for 60 minutes)

Ingredients:

½	cup	sweet potato, boiled or baked and mashed
½	cup	of coconut flour, sifted
1	tsp	sodium bicarbonate or baking soda
½	cup	raisins
3	pcs	organic eggs
1	tsp	melted butter or coconut oil
1	tbsp	lemon juice
2	tsp	cinnamon
1	tsp	vanilla

A pinch of salt

Instructions:

1. Preheat the oven at 350°F.
2. Mix all the ingredients except the raisins in a blender or a food processor. Pulse for at least 5 minutes until everything is well combined. Stir in the raisins.
3. Line a small 6" x 2.5" loaf pan with baking paper. Make sure to let the paper hang to the sides to be able to easily remove.
4. Spoon the batter onto the pan. Also use the spoon to evenly distribute the mixture.
5. Bake the raisin bread for 40 minutes.
6. Remove from oven and cover the loaf with foil. Bake for another 20 minutes.
7. Remove again from the oven and let cool for 20 minutes before slicing and serving.

Paleo Banana Cinnamon Bread With Walnuts

(Makes 1 loaf, Prep for 10 minutes, Cook for 45 minutes)

Ingredients:

2	pcs	big bananas (overripe)
2	pcs	large eggs
1 ½	cups	cashew butter
¼	cup	apple sauce
2	tbsp	maple syrup
1 ½	tsp	sodium bicarbonate or baking soda
¼	tsp	cinnamon
¼	cup	walnuts, chopped

Instructions:

1. Preheat oven at 325°F.
2. Put all the ingredients in a blender or food processor and pulse for 5 minutes until everything is blended.
3. Pour the mixture in a standard 9"x5" loaf pan (9×5).
4. Bake the banana bread for about 45 minutes or until the edges turn brown and the center is cooked. Once cooked, it tends to puff up and deflate once cooled. It's natural.
5. For best result, store in a fridge to avoid the bread from turning mushy if served early.

Paleo Garlic Buns

(Makes 1 loaf or 12 slices, Prep for 20 minutes, Cook for 40 minutes)

Ingredients:

Dry

¼	cup	of coconut flour
¾	cup	tapioca flour
½	tsp	fresh garlic, chopped
1	tsp	sea salt
½	tsp	Italian seasoning

Wet

½	cup	water
1	large	egg

Instructions:

1. Set the oven at 350°F.
2. Boil water, sea salt and olive oil in a small pan.
3. Remove the mixture from heat before adding the chopped garlic.
4. Mix in the tapioca flour and let the mixture rest for about 5 minutes.
5. Beat the eggs and add the Italian seasoning. Pour them into the mixture.
6. Add the coconut flour to the mixture and knead them into dough for a minute or 2.
7. Roll a 1" piece of dough into a small ball and place the ball on a greased baking sheet. Do the same for the rest.
8. Bake the dough for around 30-40 minutes.

Paleo Coconut Bread

(Makes 1 loaf or 12 slices, Prep for 20 minutes, Cook for 40 minutes)

Ingredients:

3	cups	coconut meat, shredded
6	med	eggs
1	tsp	baking powder
1	tsp	vanilla extract
1	tbsp	honey
1	tsp	coconut oil

Instructions

1. Set the oven at 300°F.
2. Line a regular size bread loaf pan with baking paper.
3. Combine the eggs and vanilla in a large-sized bowl and beat them until smooth.
4. In a separate bowl, mix the shredded coconut meat and the baking powder. Stir well to distribute the baking powder evenly. Add this to the large bowl with egg mixture.
5. Pour all the mixture into the lined loaf pan.
6. Bake for around 30-40 minutes. Do the toothpick or the knife test. If the center comes out clean, then it's done.
7. Remove from the oven and let cool for 20 minutes before flipping and slicing thickly.

Paleo Sweet Potato Bread

(Makes 1 loaf or 8 slices, Prep for 20 minutes, Cook for 40 minutes)

Ingredients:

1	cup	sweet potato flesh, cooked and mashed
½	cup	of coconut flour
3	large	eggs
3	tbsp	of coconut milk
1	tsp	sodium bicarbonate or baking soda
2	tbsp	lemon juice

a pinch of sea salt

Instructions:

1. Preheat the oven at 350°F. Line a regular sized loaf tin with greased baking paper. Let the paper hang over the sides to remove the bread easily.
2. Mix all the ingredients into a blender or a food processor. Pulse for 5 minutes or until everything is well blended.
3. Pour the mixture onto the loaf tin and bake for 40 minutes.
4. Remove from oven and let it cool before slicing thickly.

Paleo Lemon Glazed Lemon Bread

(Makes 1 loaf or 8 slices, Prep for 10 minutes,
Cook for 40 minutes)

Ingredients:
For the Lemon Bread

⅔	cup	of coconut flour
1	tsp	sodium bicarbonate or baking soda
6	large	eggs
¼	cup	coconut oil
2	large	lemons juiced and zest
½	cup	of coconut milk
½	cup	organic honey
¼	tsp	sea salt

For the Lemon Glaze:

2	tbsp	coconut oil
2	tbsp	organic honey
2	tbsp	of coconut milk
½	tsp	pure vanilla extract
1	pc	lemon

Instructions

For the Lemon Bread:
1. Set the oven at 350 °F. Line a bread pan with greased baking paper.
2. Zest the lemons before juicing them. Get the zest of the lemon's skin by using a grater or a zester.
3. Combine all the ingredients of the lemon loaf into a mixing bowl and mix. You can also use a food processor to mix the ingredients quickly and evenly.
4. Pour the mixture into the greased bread pan. Spread evenly.
5. Bake for 30-45 minutes until the top turns golden. Do the knife or the toothpick test to check if the center is cooked.
6. Remove from oven and set aside to cool.

Instructions for Lemon glaze:
1. While waiting for the lemon loaf to cook, combine all the lemon glaze ingredients in a small pan.
2. Turn the stove to low and wait for the mixture to boil and simmer.
3. Remove from heat and let it cool. You can put it in the fridge to make the glaze firmer.
4. Once the loaf is cooked and cooled, pour the lemon glaze on top of the loaf and spread evenly with the back of the spoon.
5. For best result, put the lemon glazed loaf in a refrigerator for at least 30 minutes before serving.

Paleo Zucchini Bread With Almonds

(Makes 1 loaf or 8 slices, Prep for 10 minutes,
Cook for 40 minutes)

Ingredients:

1 ½	cup	of almond flour
¾	cup	almond butter
1 ½	cup	zucchini, shredded and squeezed
¼	cup	arrowroot
1	large	egg
2	tbsp	coconut oil
1	tsp	sodium bicarbonate or baking soda
5	tbsp	organic honey
1	tsp	vanilla extract
1	tsp	nutmeg
1 ½	tsp	cinnamon
¼	cup	almonds (optional)

Instructions:

1. Preheat the oven up to 325°F. Grease the loaf tin with coconut oil.
2. In a large- sized bowl, beat egg. Add in coconut oil and almond butter and whisk thoroughly.
3. Put the shredded zucchini and mix well.
4. Sift the almond flour, cinnamon, baking soda and nutmeg in a separate bowl. Mix them together.
5. Gently pour the wet batter to the dry. Mix them thoroughly until they are blended nicely.
6. Transfer the zucchini bread's batter into the greased baking loaf pan.
7. Bake for approximately 60-90 minutes. Do the knife or toothpick test to check if the center is cooked.
8. Remove from the oven and let cool for at least an hour. The remaining heat will finish cooking the bread.

Paleo Garlic-Onion Bread

(Makes 1 loaf or 8 slices, Prep for 10 minutes, Cook for 40 minutes)

Ingredients:

½	cup	almond meal
½	cup	walnut meal
½	cup	flax meal
2	tsp	baking powder
2	tsp	sodium bicarbonate or baking soda
1	tsp	garlic powder
1	tsp	onion powder
½	tsp	salt
1	tbsp	sesame seeds
4	large	eggs

Instructions:

1. Preheat oven at 350°F.
2. Mix all dry ingredients in a large- sized bowl.
3. Beat eggs in a small bowl.
4. Pour the eggs in to the bowl with the dry ingredients. Mix well.
5. Pour the mixture in a small greased loaf pan.
6. Sprinkle extra sesame seeds on top.
7. Bake for 20-25 minutes.
8. Remove from oven and let it cool before slicing and serving.

Paleo Herb Bread

(Makes 1 loaf or 8 slices, Prep for 10 minutes, Cook for 40 minutes)

Ingredients:

Dry

1 ½	cups	of almond flour, blanched
2	tbsp	golden flaxseed meal
2	tbsp	of coconut flour
1	tbsp	fresh rosemary, chopped
1	tbsp	thyme, chopped
¼	tsp	sea salt
1 ½	tsp	sodium bicarbonate or baking soda

Wet

5	large	eggs
¼	cup	coconut oil
1	tbsp	vinegar (apple cider)

Instructions:

1. Preheat oven up to 350 °F. Grease a standard sized loaf pan with coconut oil.
2. Put all of the dry ingredients into a blender or food processor and pulse everything for a minute or so.
3. Beat eggs, oil and vinegar together before adding onto the food processor. Pulse again.
4. Pour everything into the greased loaf pan. Bake for 30-40 minutes. Do the toothpick test to make sure. (to prevent the top from turning into dark brown, cover the top with aluminum foil once it turns slightly golden.)
5. Remove from oven and let cool before slicing.
6. Great with grass-fed butter.

Chocolate Squash Bread

(Makes 1 loaf or 8 slices, Prep for 10 minutes,
Cook for 45 minutes)

Ingredients:

½	cup	squash flesh, cooked and mashed
½	cup	of coconut flour
½	tsp	sea salt
½	tsp	sodium bicarbonate or baking soda
5	pcs	dates, pitted, cooked and mashed
1	tbsp	vanilla extract
2	tbsp	maple syrup
¼	cup	coconut oil, melted
6	large	eggs
½	cup	chocolate chips

Instructions

1. Set oven at 350° F. Grease and line a bread pan with baking paper.
2. Prepare the dates by pitting it and putting it in a microwavable bowl with 1 tbsp of water. Heat it on high for 30 seconds and mash with a fork. Pour maple syrup to make a paste.
3. Combine coconut flour, sea salt and baking soda in a bowl.
4. In a separate small bowl, mix together the cooked squash, vanilla, eggs and the date paste. Whisk until everything is well mixed.
5. Add all the whisked wet ingredients into the dry ingredient's bowl and mix thoroughly.
6. Mix in the chocolate chips and the coconut oil.
7. Transfer the bread's batter into the grease bread pan.
8. Bake for 45 minutes.
9. Remove from the oven and put on a wire rack to cool.

Paleo Cinnamon Bread

(Makes 1 loaf or 8 slices, Prep for 10 minutes, Cook for 40 minutes)

Ingredients:

½	cup	of coconut flour
1	cup	sunflower seed butter
¼	cup	coconut sugar (granules)
3	large	eggs
1	tbsp	vinegar
½	tsp	sodium bicarbonate or baking soda
¼	tsp	salt
1	tbsp	cinnamon

Instructions:

1. Preheat oven to 350 F. Grease a regular sized loaf pan.
2. Combine coconut sugar, sunflower seed butter and eggs in a large- sized bowl.
3. Mix in the baking soda, salt and vinegar.
4. Pour the batter in the grease loaf. Spread to evenly distribute the batter.
5. In a small bowl, combine the coconut sugar granules with cinnamon.
6. Sprinkle the cinnamon mixture on top of the loaf.
7. Bake for 40 minutes.
8. Remove from the oven and let it cool for 30 minutes before slicing and serving.

Chapter 3. Paleo Muffins

Yes, you can still eat those delicious muffins while on Paleo. The following recipes will let you eat those muffins guilt-free. Ordinary commercial muffins use all-purpose flour and milk in most recipes. Creative Paleo cooks hacked some great muffin recipes to create these delicious muffins the Paleo way. They will surely save your morning cravings without adding on the weight because these recipes are totally low-carb.

So start greasing your muffin pans and start baking!

Basic Paleo Muffin
(Makes 10, Prep for 5 minutes, Cook for 18 minutes)

Ingredients

Dry
2 ½	cups	almond meal or almond flour
¾	tsp	sodium bicarbonate or baking soda
½	tsp	sea salt

Wet
⅓	cup	of any of the following: pumpkin puree, butternut squash puree, Squash puree, super ripe banana or apple sauce.
3	large	eggs
2	tbsp	honey
1	tsp	apple cider or white vinegar
2	tbsp	vegetable oil or coconut oil

Optional additional flavors of choice:
1	tsp	vanilla or almond extract, lemon or citrus zest, cinnamon or cumin spices and herbs

Optional Toppings or Stir-ins of choice:
1	cup	organic and fresh fruits (apple, blueberries, peaches)
½	cup	organic and dried fruits, chocolates or nuts (chopped nuts, almonds, macadamia)

Instructions

1. Set your oven at 350°F. In a muffin tin with 12 cups, line 10 cups with either foil or paper liners.
2. Combine almond flour, salt and baking soda in a bowl. Whisk in the dried herbs and spices if you're using any.
3. Beat the eggs in a small bowl. Add in the pumpkin (or whatever vegetable or fruits you're adding), oil, vinegar and honey. Also add in zest and juices if you're putting any.
4. Combine the wet batter to the bowl with the dry ones. Stir consistently until well blended. Add in additional stir-ins of choice.
5. Pour the batter evenly in the lined muffin cups.
6. Bake in the oven for about 18 minutes. Check if the centers are set and the edges are golden brown. Use the toothpick test. Stick a toothpick in the center and if it comes out clean, then it's done.
7. Remove the tin from the oven and place in on a wire rack. Let the muffins cool for 30 minutes before removing them from the tin.

Choco-Banana Muffins

(Makes 8, Prep for 5 minutes, Cook for 15-35 minutes)

Ingredients:

½ cup of almond flour
3 tbsp of coconut flour
¼ cup ground flax seed
2 large eggs
¼ cup carob powder melted in ¼ cup coconut oil
2 large super ripe bananas,
¼ cup coconut oil, melted
½ tsp vanilla
½ tsp sea salt
¼ cup honey

Instructions:

1. Preheat your oven upto 350°F. Grease and line a regular sized muffin pan.
2. Dissolve the carob powder with the coconut oil until it turns smooth. In a lunchbox lid, pour the mixture out and spread it to form a thin layer. Put it in the fridge for 10-15 minutes to harden.
3. Stir the ground flax seed in ¼ cup water. Set aside for a few minutes and wait for it to thicken.
4. Using a food processor or blender, mix coconut oil, mashed banana, vanilla, and honey.
5. Combine all of the wet ingredients into the bowl of the dry ones.
6. Break the frozen carob slabs into tiny pieces and mix into the batter.
7. Pour all of the muffin's batter into the greased muffin pans. Spread the batter evenly.
8. Bake the muffins for 15-35 minutes.
9. Remove from oven and let cool in a wire rack.

Strawberry Muffins

(Makes 8, Prep for 5 minutes, Cook for 20 minutes)

Ingredients

Dry ingredients:

1/3	cup	arrowroot flour
2/3	cup	of coconut flour
1/2	tsp	sea salt
1/2	tsp	ground cinnamon
1/2	tsp	baking powder
1/2	tsp	sodium bicarbonate or baking soda
1	cup	strawberries, freeze dried
1/4	cup	coconut sugar

Wet ingredients:

6	large	eggs, beaten
1	tbsp	vanilla extract
1	tsp	vinegar (apple cider)
1/4	cup	coconut oil, melted
1/3	cup	of coconut milk
1/4	cup	maple syrup

Instructions

1. Preheat the oven to 350°F. Put grease in a 12 tin muffin pan.
2. In a large- sized bowl, combine all the dry ingredients, Whisk until everything is well incorporated.
3. Get a separate bowl and beat the eggs until fluffy before adding in the remaining wet ingredients. It's recommended to melt the coconut oil first or whisk it immediately after putting it in.
4. Pour all of wet batter into the bowl with the dry ones. Place everything in a food processor or a whisk to blend the batter.
5. Allow the batter to breathe for a minute before pouring it in the greased muffin tins.
6. Bake in the oven for 20 minutes.
7. Remove the muffins from the oven and let cool completely.

Paleo Peach Muffins

(Makes 8-9, Prep for 5 minutes, Cook for 25-30 minutes)

Ingredients

Dry

2	cups	of almond flour
½	tsp	sodium bicarbonate or baking soda
⅛	tsp	sea salt

Wet

1	cup	fresh peaches, peeled and diced
3	large	eggs
2	tbsp	ghee or coconut oil, melted
2	tbsp	honey
1	tbsp	lemon juice

Instructions

1. Set the oven to 325°. Grease and line a muffin tin of 12.
2. In a large - sized bowl, put all the dry ingredients.
3. Mix all the wet ingredients except the fresh peaches in a small bowl.
4. Pour the wet ingredients into the dry ones. Mix the batter then add the fresh peaches.
5. Using an ice cream or cookie scoop, scoop the batter to fill ¾ of the muffin cups.
6. Bake in the oven for 25-30 minutes until they turn golden brown or until the toothpick comes out clean.
7. Remove from the oven and place in a wire rack to cool.

Carrot And Avocado Muffins

(Makes 6, Prep for 5 minutes, Cook for 12-15 minutes)

Ingredients:

Dry

1/3	cup	carrot, grated
¼	cup	super ripe avocado, mashed
¼	cup	of coconut flour
¼	tsp	baking powder

Wet

¼	cup	honey
1/2	tsp	lemon zest
3	large	eggs

Instructions:

1. Preheat the oven to 375 °F. Grease and line the muffin tin.
2. Beat the eggs in a large - sized bowl before adding the mashed avocado, carrot, and honey and lemon zest.
3. In a large mixing bowl, sift the coconut flour and baking powder
4. While stirring, mix the wet ingredients with the dry. You'll get a runny batter
5. Pour or spoon the muffin's batter into the cups of the greased muffin tray. Make sure it's not so full, to allow for growth.
6. Bake for 12-15 minutes.

Paleo Lemon Muffins With Poppy Seeds

(Makes 8, Prep for 5 minutes, Cook for 25-30 minutes)

Ingredients

Dry

⅓	cup	of coconut flour
1	tbsp	poppy seeds
⅛	tsp	salt
½	tsp	sodium bicarbonate or baking soda

Wet

4	large	eggs
1	pc	lemon's zest
3	tbsp	lemon juice
¼	cup	ghee or coconut oil, melted
¼	cup	honey
1	tsp	vanilla extract

Instructions

1. set oven to 325°. Grease and line a muffin tin of 12.
2. In a large - sized bowl, put all the dry ingredients.
3. Mix all the wet ingredients in a small bowl.
4. Pour the wet ingredients into the dry ones. Using an ice cream or cookie scoop, scoop the batter to fill ¾ of the muffin cups.
5. Bake in the oven for 25-30 minutes until they turn golden brown or until the toothpick comes out clean.
6. Remove from the oven and place in a wire rack to cool.

Paleo Pizza Muffin

(Makes 12, prep for 5 minutes, Cook for 20-30 minutes)

Ingredients:
Dry

¼	cup	arrowroot flour (or coconut flour)
4	cups	of almond flour
4	tbsp	ground flaxseed
1	tbsp	oregano
1	tbsp	parsley
1	tbsp	garlic powder
8	slices	fried bacon, finely chopped using a food processor
½	cup	spinach, finely chopped using a food processor
4	links	Italian sausage, finely chopped or ground using a food processor

Wet

4	eggs	
½	cup	ghee or coconut oil, melted

Instructions

1. Preheat the oven to 325°.Grease and line a muffin tin of 12.
2. In a large - sized bowl, put all the dry ingredients.
3. Mix all the wet ingredients in a small bowl.
4. Pour the wet ingredients into the dry ones. Using an ice cream or cookie scoop, scoop the batter to fill ¾ of the muffin cups.
5. Bake in the oven for 25-30 minutes until they turn golden brown or until the toothpick comes out clean.
6. Remove from the oven and place in a wire rack to cool.

Pesto Egg Muffins

(Makes 8, Prep for 5 minutes, Cook for 30 minutes)

Ingredients:

For pesto:

½	cup	Fresh basil
1/3	cup	Almonds
1	small	garlic clove
1/3	cup	Olive oil,
2	tbsp	Water

A dash of sea salt and pepper

For egg muffins –

1	med	Onion, diced
1	tbsp	Coconut oil,
2	cups	Broccoli, chopped
8	oz	Bacon
8	large	Eggs

Instructions:

1. Preheat the oven to 350°F. Grease and line a muffin tin of 12.
2. For the pesto, puree all the pesto ingredients with a food processor or a blender. Set aside. The pesto paste will be more than your needs so you can use the leftovers for toppings.
3. Heat coconut oil in a skillet over medium heat. Sauté onion for 5 minutes until translucent.
4. Stir in the bacon and broccoli for around 6 to 12 minutes until soft. Remove from heat and set aside.
5. Beat the eggs in a large - sized bowl. Combine the sautéed ingredients and the pesto. Stir everything until they forma batter.
6. Use a spoon to scoop egg mixture to fill half of each muffin cup.
7. Bake for 30 minutes or until the top turn's brown and eggs are set.
8. Remove from the oven and set to cool in a wire rack. Top it with extra pesto before serving.

Dark Chocolate And Bacon Muffins
(Makes 16-18, Prep for 5 minutes, Cook for 25-30 minutes)

Ingredients:

For the muffins
Dry

½	cup	of coconut flour
¼	cup	of almond flour
2	tsp	sodium bicarbonate or baking soda
1	tsp	baking powder
1	tsp	salt
½	cup	bacon or 12 strips
100	grams	dark chocolate
50	grams	cocoa powder
½	cup	crème fraiche
¼	cup	espresso or very strong coffee

Wet

2	large	eggs
2	tbsp	honey
½	cup	olive oil
1	cup	water

Instructions:

For the Choco-bacon:

1. In a pan, fry the bacon until its edges are brown and crispy. Remove from heat and drain oil using a paper towel.
2. In a small pan, melt the dark chocolate.
3. Crush the crispy slices of bacon and spread the crumbles around the baking tray lined with baking paper. Pour the melted chocolate over the top of the bacon. Leave the Choco-bacon to harden.

For the muffin:

4. Preheat the oven to 370°F. Grease and line a muffin tin of 12 or 16.
5. Use large bowl and mix all of the dry ingredients.
6. Beat the eggs in a separate bowl. Add the coffee, crème fraiche olive oil and honey. Pour this mixture into the dry ingredients. Stir well until everything is well mixed. Add water to make the batter more watery like cookie dough because coconut flour takes in moisture.
7. Break the choco-bacon chips and stir it in the batter.
8. Pour the batter in the prepared muffin tin.
9. Bake the muffins for 30 minutes until toothpick comes out clean.
10. Remove from the oven and let cool before popping out the muffins from the tin.

Chicken Egg Muffin
(Makes 6, Prep for 30 minutes, Cook for 30 minutes)

Ingredients:

For the chicken:

1	cup	chicken breast, deboned and shredded
½	tsp	garlic
¼	tsp	sea salt
¼	tsp	black pepper
6	large	eggs, whisked
2	tbsp	onion, diced

Instructions:
1. Preheat the oven to 425°F. Line the muffin tin cups with parchment paper.
2. Place the chicken breast on a baking pan. Season with garlic, black pepper and sea salt. Bake for 25 minutes.
3. Remove from oven and set aside.
4. Beat the eggs in a small whisking bowl. Add and whisk the green onion, black pepper and sea salt.
5. Pour the egg mixture half way through the muffin cups. Scoop 1 spoon of the shredded chicken and evenly distribute it on top of the muffin egg batter.
6. Bake for 30 minutes until the muffin's edges turn golden brown.

Dark Choco-Zucchini Muffins
(Makes 8-10 muffins, Prep for 10 minutes,
Cook for 25-30 minutes)

Ingredients:
Dry

½	cup	of almond flour
¼	cup	coconut flour
1	tbsp	tapioca flour
1	tsp	sodium bicarbonate or baking soda
1	cup	zucchini, grated
3.5	oz	dark chocolate, chopped
¼	cup	cocoa powder
¼	tsp	salt

Wet

¼	cup	organic honey
¼	cup	ghee, melted
4	large	eggs
¼	cup	of coconut milk
1	tbsp	vanilla extract

Instructions:

1. Set the oven to 350°F. Grease and line a regular sized muffin pan with paper liners.
2. Beat the eggs in a large - sized bowl and whisk in melted ghee. Pour in the honey, coconut milk and vanilla. Whisk thoroughly to combine well.
3. Get a separate bowl and sift the dry ingredients, the flours, baking soda, cocoa powder and salt.
4. Put the dry ingredients in the large bowl with the wet ones.
5. Stir in the grated zucchini and half of the dark chocolate chunks.
6. Use a spoon to transfer the muffin's batter into the lined muffin cups. Sprinkle the top with the remaining chocolate chunks.
7. Bake in the oven for 25-30 minutes, test if the toothpick comes out clean
8. Remove from oven and. Let the muffins cool for 5 to 10 minutes in the tin before removing the muffins to cool in the rack.

Chapter 4. Paleo Biscuits

Biscuits can really come in handy when you're on the go. They are also great for side snacks and in-between meals or when your meal falls short. It's great to have biscuits to complement with chilies, soups, and chicken dishes of all kinds. A cup of coffee would be lonely without some of these biscuits to pair with.

Simple Paleo Biscuits
(Makes 12 biscuits, Prep for 5 minutes, Cook for 15 minutes)

Ingredients
⅔	Cup	coconut flour
1	tsp	baking powder
½	tsp	salt
½	cup	coconut oil, melted
6	large	eggs
2	tbsp	honey

Instructions:

1. Preheat oven at 400°F. Grease cookie sheet spread on a baking pan.
2. In a small bowl, mix together all the dry ingredients.
3. In a large-sized bowl, beat the eggs before adding the honey.
4. Add the dry ingredients to the large bowl and mix thoroughly.
5. Scoop a spoonful of batter and drop onto the cookie sheet. Wet your finger with water and shape the batter/dough into small disks. You can fit 12 small biscuits in a regular size baking pan.
6. Bake in the oven for 12-15 minutes until the top turns golden brown.
7. Remove from oven and let cool.

Chives Paleo Biscuits

(Makes 5, Prep for 5 minutes, Cook for 10 minutes)

Ingredients:

¼	cup	coconut flour
1	cup	of almond flour
1	tsp	honey
¼	cup	chives, chopped
1	tsp	sodium bicarbonate or baking soda
1	tsp	sea salt
3	tbsp	ghee
3	large	eggs

Instructions

1. Preheat oven to 325°F.
2. Using a blender or a food processor, puree the chives. Or simply chop them finely.
3. Mix the eggs and pulse again.
4. Add the flours, salt and baking soda. Pulse again.
5. Drop in the ghee while the food processor is blending. The batter is supposed to be firm.
6. Scoop 2 tbsp of batter onto the cookie sheet on an aluminum baking pan. Flat the dough to form it into biscuit shape. Do this for the rest of the batter.
7. Smooth out the biscuits by dipping your hand in a bow of water and run circles over the biscuits.
8. Bake for about 22-25 minutes until they turn slightly brown.
9. Remove from oven and let cool before serving.

Garlic Biscuits

(Makes 8-10 biscuits, Prep for 10, Cook for 25)

Ingredients:

¼	cup	coconut flour
1	cup	of almond flour
1	tsp	honey
¼	cup	garlic, chopped
3	tbsp	ghee
3	large	eggs
1	tsp	sodium bicarbonate or baking soda
1	tsp	sea salt

Instructions

1. Preheat oven to 325°F.
2. Using a blender or a food processor, puree the garlic.
3. Mix the eggs and pulse again.
4. Add the flours, salt and baking soda. Pulse again.
5. Drop in the ghee while the food processor is blending. The batter is supposed to be firm.
6. Scoop 2 tbsp of batter onto the cookie sheet on a baking pan. Flat the dough to form it into biscuit shape. Do this for the rest of the batter.
7. Smooth out the biscuits by dipping your hand in a bow of water and run circles over the biscuits.
8. Bake for about 22-25 minutes until they turn slightly brown.
9. Remove from oven and let cool before serving.

Onion Biscuits

(Makes 8-10 biscuits, Prep for 10, Cook for 25)

Ingredients

1	cup	of almond flour
¼	cup	coconut flour
1	tsp	honey
2	med	onions, roasted
3	tbsp	ghee
3	large	eggs
1	tsp	sodium bicarbonate or baking soda
1	tsp	sea salt

Instructions

1. Preheat oven to 325°F.
2. Using a blender or a food processor, puree the onions.
3. Mix the eggs and pulse again.
4. Add the flours, salt and baking soda. Pulse again.
5. Drop in the ghee while the food processor is blending. The batter is supposed to be firm.
6. Scoop 2 tbsp of batter onto the cookie sheet on a baking pan. Flat the dough to form it into biscuit shape. Do this for the rest of the batter.
7. Smooth out the biscuits by dipping your hand in a bow of water and run circles over the biscuits.
8. Bake for about 22-25 minutes until they turn slightly brown.
9. Remove from oven and let cool before serving.

Paleo 3-Flour Biscuits

(Makes 8-10 biscuits, Prep for 10, Cook for 12-14 minutes)

Ingredients
Dry
2/3	cup	tapioca flour
1	cup	of almond flour
½	cup	coconut flour
1	tsp	sodium bicarbonate or baking soda
2	tsp	baking powder
¼	tsp	sea salt

Wet
5	tbsp	Grass-fed Butter cold,
½	cup	of coconut milk
1	tsp	lemon juice
2	large	eggs

Instructions

1. Preheat oven to 400°F. Line a baking sheet with cookie sheet.
2. Combine all the 3 flours, baking soda, baking powder and salt in a large mixing bowl.
3. Mix in the grass-fed butter to the dry ingredients. The batter will resemble a coarse meal. Use your hands to make a well in the center of the mixture.
4. In a separate bowl, whisk the coconut milk and the lemon juice together. Set for a few minutes. Crack an egg in the bowl and whisk everything until frothy.
5. Pour the wet ingredients into the well created from the dry ingredients. Use a rubber spatula to fold the dough/batter until everything is well combined.
6. Let it sit for another 5 minutes to let the flour absorb the moisture.
7. After setting it for a few minutes, the dough will not be as sticky and wet as in the beginning.
8. Scoop dough and shape it into balls. Flatten the balls into sphere shapes.
9. Sprinkle the dough with tapioca starch to prevent it from being sticky. Repeat the process for the remaining dough.
10. Place the biscuit dough in the cookie sheet. They should have enough space to grow.
11. Bake in the oven for 12-14 minutes.
12. Remove from oven and cool on a wire rack.

Spicy Cauliflower And Bacon Biscuit
(Makes 8-10 biscuits, Prep for 10, Cook for 35)

Ingredients:

Dry

½	cup	of almond flour
1/2	tsp	garlic powder
1/2	tsp	sea salt
1	cup	cauliflower florets
½	cup	crispy bacon, cooked and chopped
½	tsp	black pepper
1	pc	jalapeño, chopped (seeds removed)

Wet

2	tbsp	virgin olive oil
2	large	eggs

Instructions:

1. Preheat the oven to 400°F. Line a baking sheet with parchment paper.
2. Shred the cauliflower with a food processor.
3. In a large skillet, heat olive oil over medium heat.
4. Heat the olive oil in a large skillet over medium heat.
5. Sauté the jalapeño, shredded cauliflower, bacon, sea salt and black pepper for about 7 minutes or until the vegetable is done. Remove the mixture from heat.
6. In a large-sized bowl, beat the eggs. Add in the of almond flour. Gently pour the sautéed mixture in the bowl. Stir until everything is well mixed.
7. Scoop the dough with a ¼ sized measuring cup powdered with almond flour. Gently pop the batter out in the lined parchment paper by tapping the bottom of the cup. Make sure it all comes out clean.
8. Bake in the oven for 35-40 minutes, or until they turn golden brown.
9. Remove from oven and allow cooling on the sheet for 10 minutes.

Chapter 5. Paleo Waffles

Some people's mornings will not be complete without waffles. Unlike pancakes, this thick and light flour food is supposed to be crisp on the outside while soft on the inside. The batter is almost the same as pancakes but the difference is the process. Waffles are baked using a waffle iron or an electric waffle maker to give a crisscross pattern on both sides.

Contrary to popular belief, you can still eat waffles on Paleo diet. All of the following waffle recipes will feel like cheating but you're still on the Paleo track. Enjoy these delicious waffles and their sweet fruit syrups without feeling a little bit of remorse.

Simple Paleo Waffles
(Makes 5, Prep for 5 minutes, Cook for 10 minutes)

Ingredients:
Dry

½	cup	tapioca flour
½	cup	of coconut flour
¼	tsp	sea salt
½	tsp	sodium bicarbonate or baking soda
½	tsp	baking powder

Wet

1	cup	of coconut milk
1	tsp	vinegar

3	large	eggs
2	tbsp	coconut oil, melted
1	tsp	vanilla extract

Instructions:

1. Pour the apple cider vinegar in the coconut milk and set aside for 5 minutes.
2. Set the waffle iron by preheating it. Brush it with coconut oil to prevent it from sticking.
3. Crack the eggs in a blender or a food processor and beat for a few seconds until smooth. Pour the soured coconut milk and pulse again.
4. Mix in the rest of the ingredients. The batter is supposed to be thin yet not so watery.
5. Pour the batter enough to fill the waffle maker.
6. Wait until the light goes off. To check if it's done, it should turn golden brown.
7. Repeat this process to the rest of the batter.

Chocolate Waffles

(Makes 5 waffles, Prep for 5 minutes, Cook for 15 minutes)

Ingredients
For the waffle

4	tbsp	of coconut flour
1	cup	of almond flour
½	tsp	sodium bicarbonate or baking soda
¼	tsp	sea salt
4	tbsp	cocoa powder
¼	cup	dark chocolate chips
1	cup	apple sauce
4	large	eggs
½	tsp	vanilla

For the chocolate sauce

¼	cup	dark chocolate chips
2	tbsp	coconut oil

Instructions

For the chocolate waffle
1. Preheat the waffle maker to high.
2. Mix all the waffle's ingredients together in a blender of a food processor. Blend until everything is well combined.
3. Scoop ¾ cups of batter and pour it into your waffle maker.
4. Cook the waffles for around 4 - 5 minutes. Check if it turns brown.
5. Remove the waffle from the waffle maker and repeat the process for the rest of the batter.

For the Chocolate Sauce
1. Combine dark chocolate chips with coconut oil in a saucepan.
2. Heat it over low fire. Stir until everything is melted.
3. Remove from heat and pour over waffles.

Nutty Caramelized Apple Waffles

(Makes 4-6 waffles, Prep for 15 minutes, Cook for 20 minutes)

Ingredients:

For the waffles

Dry

¼	cup	of coconut flour
¼	cup	raw pecans
¾	tsp	sodium bicarbonate or baking soda
¾	cup	macadamia nuts or raw cashews
¼	tsp	sea salt

Wet

3	large	eggs
¼	cup	of coconut milk
3	tbsp	coconut oil, melted
2	tbsp	honey

For the Caramelized Apple Syrup

1	cup	apples, diced
¼	cup	of coconut milk
3	tbsp	ghee
¼	cup	honey

A pinch of sea salt

Instructions:

For the Waffles
1. Preheat the waffle iron over high heat.
2. Use a blender or a food processor to mix the milk, pecans, eggs, nuts, honey, and melted coconut oil. Pulse until everything is very smooth and creamy. To ensure a smooth blend, stop the blender and use a spatula to push down the mixture from the sides.
3. In a large- sized bowl, combine the dry ingredients such as the coconut flour, baking soda and salt.
4. Gradually add the dry ingredients to the blender and pulse now and then for about 30 seconds until the batter is formed.
5. Spray the waffle maker with oil before pouring ¾ cup of waffle batter into the waffle maker. Just cover the bottom portion of the waffle iron.
6. For about 45 minutes, cook the waffles and repeat the process for the rest of the batter.
7. Best to serve hot with the apple syrup.

For the Syrup

8. In a skillet, melt the butter over medium heat.
9. Whisk in the honey and bring the mixture to boil. Once it boils, reduce heat and let it simmer for 1 minute.
10. Mix in the apples and sauté it for 15 minutes. Bring again to a boil. Simmer for 5 minutes.
11. Remove the caramelized apple from heat and set to cool and thicken. Pour over the waffles.

Strawberry Chocolate Waffles

(Makes 2 waffles, Prep for 3 minutes, cook for 5minutes)

Ingredients:

Dry

1 ½	tbsp	tapioca flour
1	tbsp	ground flax seed
1	tbsp	unsweetened cocoa powder
¼	tsp	sodium bicarbonate or baking soda
½	tsp.	Vanilla extract
3	tbsp	almond milk
1	large	egg
¼	cup	strawberries, chopped fine

Instructions:

1. In a large- sized bowl, sift and whisk tapioca starch, flax seed, cocoa powder, and baking soda.
2. Beat the egg and mix in the egg and almond milk.
3. Pour the wet batter to the dry ingredients and mix thoroughly. The batter is supposed to look like a smooth brownie batter. Just add a little almond milk if it still look thick.
4. Stir in the strawberries.
5. Turn on your waffle iron and brush with coconut oil.
6. Once hot, pour in ¼ cup batter. Spread it out to cover all the bottom part of the waffle maker.
7. Close lid of the waffle maker and wait for it to cook for 3-5 minutes.

8. Repeat the process to the rest of the batter.
9. Serve with topped strawberries or chocolate.

Paleo Vanilla Waffles With Cinnamon

(Makes 5, Prep for 5 minutes, Cook for 10 minutes)

Ingredients

½   cup   of coconut flour (plus a little more)
8   large   eggs
½   cup   coconut oil, melted
1   tsp   cinnamon
1   tsp   vanilla
½   tsp   salt

Instructions

1. Preheat the waffle maker on high and grease it.
2. Mix all the ingredients in a large- sized bowl or use a food processor to combine them well.
3. The batter is supposed to be thick.
4. Scoop ¼ cup of the batter and pour it to fill the bottom part of the waffle maker.
5. Cook the waffle for about 3 minutes until it turns light brown.

Paleo Pumpkin Waffles

(Makes 6 waffles, Prep for 5 minutes, Cook for 5 minutes)

Ingredients

½	cup	of coconut flour, sifted
1 ½	tsp	cinnamon
½	tsp	sodium bicarbonate or baking soda
½	tsp	nutmeg
¼	tsp	ginger
¼	tsp	sea salt

A pinch of cloves

Wet

1	cup	pumpkin puree
¾	cup	of coconut milk, canned, unsweetened, full fat
¾	cup	apple sauce
6	large	eggs, separated
6	tbsp	ghee, melted
1	tsp	vanilla extract

Instructions

1. Preheat the waffle maker over low/medium heat. Grease it with coconut oil.
2. Combine and sift all the dry ingredients together in a large mixing bowl.
3. Separate the egg yolks in one bowl and the whites in another.
4. Put all the wet ingredients in the bowl with the egg yolks. Whisk until thoroughly blended.
5. Mix the wet batter to the dry and use a blender to smooth the batter.
6. Whip the egg whites for about 3—5 minutes until it peaks
7. Gently fold the egg whites into the waffle batter. Be careful not to flatten the fluffy egg whites.
8. Scoop just enough batter and spread it from the center of mold. Avoid overfilling as the batter might spread out.
9. Cook the waffles for about 5 minutes and repeat the whole process with remaining batter.

Macadamia Waffles In Fruit Syrup

(Makes 6 waffles, Prep for 5 minutes, Cook for 10 minutes)

Ingredients:

For the waffles
Dry

4	tbsp	of coconut flour
1	cup	macadamia nuts
¾	tsp	sodium bicarbonate or baking soda
¼	tsp	salt

Wet

3	large	eggs
3	tbsp	honey or maple syrup
½	tsp	vanilla extract
½	cup	of coconut milk
3	tbsp	milk (coconut)
3	tbsp	coconut oil, melted

For the Fruit Syrup

¼	cup	honey
1	cup	peaches, pitted and sliced into cubes
½	tsp	vanilla extract
½	tsp	lemon juice
1	cup	plums, pitted and sliced into cubes
½	cup	cherries, pitted (frozen or fresh)

Instructions:

For the syrup,

1. Combine all the syrup's ingredients in a sauce pan over medium heat. Bring it to a boil and turn the heat down to low. Let it simmer while you prepare the waffles. When syrup thickens, set aside.

For the waffles

2. Preheat a waffle iron by turning it to low.
3. Mix all the wet ingredients in a bowl. In a separate bowl, sift all of the dry ingredients
4. Combine all of the waffle's ingredients in a blender or a food processor. Make sure to put the wet ingredients first before the dry ones.
5. Blend on low to medium for around 30 seconds or until the batter turns smooth.
6. Scoop around ¼ cup of batter and pour into the waffle iron.
7. Cook the waffles on low setting for a minute. You can determine that it's done when the steam stops rising from the waffle maker.
8. Release the waffles by using a fork. Do the same process for the rest of the batter.
9. Serve with the fruit syrup on top.

Paleo Waffles In Peach Syrup

(Makes 4 waffles, Prep for 5 minutes, Cook for 10-15 minutes)

Ingredients:

For the waffles

Dry

4	tbsp	tapioca flour
1	tbsp	of coconut flour
½	cup	of almond flour
½	tsp	sodium bicarbonate or baking soda
¼	tsp	salt

Wet

1	tbsp	oil
1	tsp	vanilla
2	large	eggs

For the Peach syrup

1	cup	peach, sliced
3	tbsp	ghee or grass-fed butter
2	tbsp	maple syrup

Instructions:

For the waffles
1. Turn on your waffle maker to medium. Grease it with coconut oil.
2. Combine all the flours, baking soda and salt in a big bowl.
3. In a separate bowl, whisk the wet ingredients before pouring them over the dry ones. Mix the batter until it becomes frothy. Set it aside for 5 minutes to thicken.
4. Scoop ¼ cup of batter and pour over the waffle iron. Spread evenly.
5. Cook for 3 minutes.
6. Repeat the process for the rest of the batter.

For the peach syrup
1. Warm the peaches in a small saucepan over low heat for 5 minutes until they release some juices. Stir every once in a while
2. Take off of heat before it thickens.
3. Stir in ghee or butter and the maple syrup. Let it settle for 5 minutes.
4. Pour on top of the waffles.

Chapter 6. Paleo Pancakes

If you've just started doing Paleo Diet, you can still continue your weekend tradition of waking up with some pancakes for breakfast. These recipes will help you still feel nostalgic yet healthy and still on the Paleo track. You won't feel like cheating because the ingredients used in these recipes are totally Paleo. Fill your mornings with these guilt-free Paleo pancakes and go about your day without feeling any remorse.

Paleo Pumpkin Pancakes

(Makes 12 small pancakes, Prep for 5 minutes, Cook for 15 minutes)

Ingredients
Dry

2	tbsp	of coconut flour
1	tbsp	ground flax seed
½	cup	of almond flour
¼	tsp	sodium bicarbonate or baking soda
½	tbsp	cinnamon
1	tsp	pumpkin pie spice
¼	tsp	sea salt

Wet

½	cup	pumpkin puree
¾	cup	egg whites
2	tbsp	honey
½	tsp	vanilla
¼	cup	coconut oil for cooking pancakes

Instructions

1. Mix all all the flours, baking soda, salt and all of the dry ones in a bowl.
2. Beat the eggs and mix in other wet ingredients in a separate bowl.
3. Pour the wet ingredients to dry ingredients and mix to form a smooth batter.
4. Heat a pan or a pancake griddle over medium heat. Grease the pan with coconut oil.
5. Scoop ¼ cup of batter and pour it into the pan. If the batter is thick, help spread it into a pancake shape,
6. Cook the first side for 3-4 minutes until the bubbles turn dry or the edges are browning.
7. Flip and cook the other side for another 1-2 minutes. Repeat the process with the remaining batter. Add more coconut oil to the pan if needed.

Coco Pancakes With Pineapple Syrup

(Makes 5, Prep for 5 minutes, Cook for 10 minutes)

Ingredients

For Coconut Pancakes

Dry

½	cup	of coconut flour
½	cup	shredded coconut
1	tsp	baking powder
1/8	tsp	sea salt

Wet

3	large	eggs
1	cup	of coconut milk
2	tsp	pure vanilla extract
¼	cup	Coconut oil

For the Pineapple Syrup

1	cup	water
1	cup	honey
1 ¾	cup	dried pineapple

Instructions:

For the Coconut Pancakes

1. Beat the eggs and mix in the wet ingredients. Pour it in a blender.
2. Add in the dry ingredients and turn the food processor or the blender on high until everything is fully combined. Push down the sides of the container once or twice.
3. Let the mixture sit and thicken for 5 minutes.
4. Heat a pan or a pancake griddle over medium heat. Grease the pan with coconut oil.
5. Scoop ¼ cup of batter and pour it into the pan. If the batter is thick, help spread it into a pancake shape,
6. Cook the first side for 3-4 minutes until the bubbles turn dry or the edges are browning.
7. Flip and cook the other side for another 1-2 minutes. Repeat the process with the remaining batter. Add more coconut oil to the pan if needed.
8. Top with the pineapple syrup and sprinkle shredded coconut.

For Pineapple Syrup

9. Mix and heat all the ingredients in a saucepan over medium heat.
10. Bring to a boil and simmer for 3-5 minutes until syrup thickens and the pineapples are soft.
11. Remove from heat and let cool before storing in a clean jar.
12. Best to serve warm over hot pancakes.

Cinnamon Coco-Bane Pancakes

(Makes 12 small pancakes, Prep for 5 minutes, Cook for 15 minutes)

Ingredients:

Dry

1½	tbsp	of coconut flour
½	tsp	cinnamon
¼	tsp	sodium bicarbonate or baking soda
1	pinch	sea salt
2	large	eggs

Wet

3	tbsp	of coconut milk
2	tbsp	ripe banana, mashed
½	tsp	vinegar (apple cider)
½	tsp	vanilla extract

Coconut oil (for frying)

Instructions

1. Beat the eggs and mix in the wet ingredients. Pour it in a blender.
2. Add in the dry ingredients and turn the food processor or the blender on high until everything is fully combined. Push down the sides of the container once or twice.
3. Let the mixture sit and thicken for 5 minutes.
4. Heat a pan or a pancake griddle over medium heat. Grease the pan with coconut oil.
5. Scoop ¼ cup of batter and pour it into the pan. If the batter is thick, help spread it into a pancake shape,
6. Cook the first side for 3-4 minutes until the bubbles turn dry or the edges are browning.
7. Flip and cook the other side for another 1-2 minutes. Repeat the process with the remaining batter. Add more coconut oil to the pan if needed.

Blueberry Paleo Pancakes
(Makes 3 pancakes, Prep for 5minutes, Cook for 10 minutes)

Ingredients
3	large	egg whites, beaten
1	Tbsp	almond butter
1	piece	banana
20	pcs	blueberries
½	tsp	cinnamon

Instructions
1. Preheat skillet or pan on medium. grease with coconut oil
2. Mix egg whites, blueberries, banana and almond butter. mix well
3. Scoop ¼ cup of batter and pour into pan,
4. Cover the pan with lid.
5. Cook pancake for 2-3 min
6. Flip pancake when bubbles dry and brown the other side
7. Sprinkle with cinnamon.

Chocolate Banana Pancakes

(Makes 5 pancakes, Prep for 5 minutes, Cook for 10 minutes)

Ingredients:

Dry

½	cup	of coconut flour
1	med	super ripe banana
1	tbsp	cocoa powder
¼	tsp	sea salt
½	tsp	sodium bicarbonate or baking soda

Wet

½	cup	sun butter
½	tsp	vanilla
½	cup	water
2	large	eggs
1	tbsp	coconut oil for greasing the pan

Instructions:

1. Mix all vinegar (apple cider) bowl.
2. Beat the eggs and mix in other wet ingredients in a separate bowl.
3. Pour the wet ingredients to dry ingredients and mix to form a smooth batter.
4. Heat a pan or a pancake griddle over medium heat. Grease the pan with coconut oil.
5. Scoop ¼ cup of batter and pour it into the pan. If the batter is thick, help spread it into a pancake shape,
6. Cook the first side for 3-4 minutes until the bubbles turn dry or the edges are browning.
7. Flip and cook the other side for another 1-2 minutes. Repeat the process with the remaining batter. Add more coconut oil to the pan if needed.

Conclusion

Thank you again for purchasing this book!

I hope this book was able to help you to prepare, bake and cook gluten-free and dairy free Paleo bread, waffles, pancakes, biscuits and muffins in quick and easy steps. Rest assured, these recipes conform to the Paleo Diet instructions.

For those who are just trying out the Paleo lifestyle, I hope this book encouraged you to continue with the diet. This book simply debunks the wrong notions that Paleo restricts dieters to eat all the good and delicious foods. For bread lovers, do not hesitate to join the Paleo tribe because with these recipes, you can now enjoy the health benefits of Paleo without losing the foods you love.

The next step is to create your own recipe using these to make flour-based foods depending on your taste. Have fun baking and improving the taste of Paleo food.

Thank you and good luck!
http://paleohealthyliving.com/

Made in the USA
Lexington, KY
06 October 2018